A NEW CREATION MODEL

QUENCY GARDNER

A NEW CREATION MODEL
© COPYRIGHT 2024 BY QUENCY GARDNER

ISBN: 978-1-965498-40-8

All Scripture quotations, unless noted otherwise, are from the King James Version.

All rights reserved solely by the author. The author guarantees all contents are original and do not infringe upon the legal rights of any other person or work. No part of this book may be reproduced in any form without the permission of the author except in the case of brief quotations embodied in church-related publications, quoted portions attributed to the author, critical articles or reviews.

The views expressed in this work are solely those of the author and do not necessarily reflect the views of the publisher, and the publisher disclaims any responsibility for them.

To order additional copies of this book, contact:

Simply Best Reads LLC
39-67 58th Street, 1st floor
Woodside, NY 11377, USA
Phone: (+1 888-203-7688)
simplybestreads.com

TABLE OF CONTENTS

PREVIEW -- 1
ESTABLISHING PREMISES: -------------------------------------- 4
GOD'S CREATION THE 1ST DAY -------------------------------- 12
GOD'S CREATION THE 2ND DAY -------------------------------- 18
GOD'S CREATION THE 3RD DAY -------------------------------- 25
GOD'S CREATION THE 4TH DAY -------------------------------- 32
TRANSLATION EXPLANATION -------------------------------- 36
A VERBAL SKETCH --- 41
PROBLEMS WITH THIS MODEL ------------------------------ 50

PREVIEW

FIVE PREMISES:

1. Gen. 1:1 – The summarization of when Who did what.
2. Gen. 1:2 thru 5 – **1st Day:** Pre-earth portrait no shape, no pattern, no structure. The 1st day's creation occupants were darkness, waters and light.
3. Gen. 1:6 thru 8 – **2nd Day:** The creation of the universe – the empty heaven(s).
4. Gen. 1:9 thru 13 – **3rd Day:** The creation of the earth & some living systems.
5. Gen. 1:14 thru 19 – **4th Day:** The creation of all stellar systems, the galaxies & all that is in the universe; all that is in the Heavens (everything in outer space).

This model's design is based upon a Literal-Normal reading of Genesis one. Genesis 1:1 is a summary statement defining "when Who did what." A simplistic summation of verse one is to say, "In the beginning God created everything," and then continue with the rest of the chapter. That statement summarizes the creation account, and can be referred to as a condensed description of the rest of the chapter. Genesis 1:2 & 3 provide a pre-earth description of everything created on day-1, with a specific exclusion of the earth. Genesis 1:6 is a reference to the creation of the universal heaven – [i.e. the universal expanse – and not what some have called the atmospheric section of earth. (The rationale for this statement is explained in the chapter titled "God's Creation The 2nd Day".) If we posit the "waters" (of day-1) as the earth, we would also be saying that the huge expanse, that God called Heaven (which on day-4 will hold the astronomical bodies) was placed in the middle of the earth and that would mean that each half of the earth is on opposite sides of the universe.] Verses 9 & 10 the earth is created; the spherical formation of the earth, if the waters were not a sphere previously; the waters were separated and the land mass created. Verses 14 thru 18 describe the creation of the heavenly bodies. Although it is unknown to us exactly when the angelic entities were created. Perhaps we can assume that they were created during the creation week, provided we hold to the view that Genesis is an account of the beginning of all of creation. Genesis 2:1 seems to indicate that everything that God created, was done during the creation week. Chapter 2:1 states the following: "Thus the heavens and the earth were finished, **and all the host of them**." In that the word "heavens" is plural, this seems to imply that the heaven where God dwells did not exist before God created it (during the creation week) as well as "all the host of them." (As a note: When God was making the universe, He built within this system certain operational parameters, some of which we have defined as the "laws of physics." That being said, I think it is okay to determine when certain parameters were possibly established. Therefore, on occasion, I will make comments about such. Realizing that such are only speculations.)

ESTABLISHING PREMISES:

PRE-CREATION RHETORICAL QUESTIONS

1. Before creation, was there such a thing as "physical space?"
2. Does God need space to exist in? – Is God non-spatial?
3. Before God (the God-Head) created anything, what actually exist?
4. Was there a time when God's throne did not exist?

> **Genesis 1:1**
> ¹In the beginning God created the heavens and the earth.

I would like to provide two reasonable statements, with which to use as presuppositions. **1.** Everything God created, was designed for a specific purpose, even if we (up to this date) have not understood its purpose. **2.** When God identifies what He created by giving it a descriptive name, <u>such should be understood that it was created for that named purpose</u>.

Genesis one is referred to as the creation model. Each day of creation provides additional details to this creation model. We can begin framing this model based on the descriptions provided to us as we progress thru each text. When I began an in-depth examination of Genesis 1:1, I proposed two options of interpretation for the first verse.

Establishing Premises

Option-1: Genesis 1:1 may be a description of what God created on the 1st day. **Option-2:** Or Genesis 1:1 maybe a summary statement of "when Who did what." I had to determine which of the two options this text is describing. This rationale helped me through the process when viewing the first verse as "a description of what God created on the 1st day." In accepting the assumption of the first option, I had to conclude that God created both the heavens and the earth on the first day. In that there is no Hebrew word for "universe," the implication of this assumption is that all of the heavens and the earth were completed on Day-1. Interpreting verse one in this manner placed me in conflict with the additional elements of creation specified (beginning with verse 2) for "day 1 thru day 4." Therefore, I had to dismiss the supposition of option-1. Next, I viewed verse one as a summary statement of "when Who did what." With the same additional elements of creation, which chapter one provides, I was able to select the "(IBE) Inference to the Best Explanation." Therefore, I determined the better fit, was the second option.

Now if my assertion is true, that Genesis 1:1 is a summarization of creation, it would follow that neither the heavens nor the earth was created on day-1. Also, in a decisive manner, this falsifies the "Gap Theory." Take note that verse one is not a testimony of that which God created on the first day. Because "Heaven" was not created on the 1st day. It is verse six which gives us the historical account on day 2 for the creation of the "heaven". The assumption has been (by some) that the heavens and the earth were created on day-1, yet verse six refutes that postulation. In that, on day 2 God said, "Let there be a firmament in the midst of the waters...". Therefore, with day-2 clearly being the day stated for the creation of the Heaven (that would mean), there would be no "Gap of time" between verses one and two. Not only so but our options would be limited <u>when applying a meaning that is contextual to the creation account</u> for the Hebrew words "tohuw (without form)," accompanied by "bohuw (void)." We would then have to use definitions, for these two words, that would be contextual to the creation account ... not to a recreation account or not to a renovation account. Someone may ask, what exactly do I mean by that? What I mean is that we have an option of two assumptions when we attempt to interpret Genesis one. Assumption #1: We can assume that Genesis one is indeed describing the actual beginning of creation. (Or) Assumption #2: We can assume that it is not actually the beginning of creation. If we go with assumption #2, we will find ourselves "out of sync" with Jesus' definition of the beginning. (For Jesus stated in Mark 10:6 "But from the beginning of the creation God made them male and female.") My assumption is that God was indeed describing the beginning. When we accept the parameters that Jesus expressed in Mark 10, "...from the beginning of the creation..." We would draw a conclusion, that God did not create the heaven of heavens first (& angels), then after a long period of time, He came up with an idea to create additional things billions of years later or even just a few years later. I would like to suggest the following as a possibility. Everything that was created, were created/made during the six days of creation. All things whether they are heavenly creatures, earthly creatures, things physical and nonphysical, as well as those things which are visible and invisible, were created during that six-day period. Genesis 2:1 can be taken as God affirming the completion of creation as described in chapter one, "Thus the heavens and the earth were finished, and all the host of them." It is again restated in Exodus 20:11. This repeats the duration of time it took for God to create / make everything. "For in six days the Lord made the heaven and the earth,..." I do not think that I would be in error to use the text from Col. 1:16 in the following manner: "For by him were all things created, that are in heaven, and that are in earth, visible and invisible, whether *they be* thrones, or dominions, or principalities, or powers: all things were created by him,..." (if I may suggest) during the creation week. <u>God began creation in the sequential order that is stated in Genesis one</u>. Therefore, it seems reasonable to conclude that the one most likely interpretation of Genesis 1:2 is that the earth (& the heaven) did not exist on day-1. For an earth, that is described as being without form is more likely to be an earth with no physical shape, no pattern and no structure – in other words, the earth did not exist. Allow me to ask you the following rhetorical question. What would an earth without a form look like? It would look like an earth that is not there. This is a "pre-earth" description. Therefore, verse 2 appears to be presenting a pre-earth description in which God, had only created Darkness and Waters. Afterward, (that is to say, twelve hours later being part of the same day), God created light … on the first day.

    I want to address, in a more detailed way, the possible concerns and thoughts by some that "waters & darkness" came into existence in a different way than by God's spoken word. If there are no issues with accepting Genesis one as the true account of the beginning of creation, then I can provide a reasonable explanation. The Scriptures do not state that God said, "let there be waters" or "let there be darkness." Yet I think it is reasonable to say that God caused Waters & Darkness to be created by the same creative process as He did for Light, through His spoken word. There are statements about creation found documented throughout the Scriptures. One such location is Hebrews 11:3 "…the worlds were framed by the **word of God**." Although we, at times, identify the "Word of God" as being Jesus, and such is true. Yet there are also times when the word of God is spoken by the Father and/or by the Son, and yet we can still say it was His spoken word. Also Psalms 33:6 & 9 presents additional information concerning the creation account, "…by the **word of the Lord**, were the heavens made … For He spake, and it was done; He commanded and it stood fast." This would strongly imply that God spoke "Darkness and Waters" into existence. He created these with His spoken words. This is further confirmed in Isaiah 45:7 "I form the light, and create darkness..." Although this text is uttering the words, "I form the light," we find a more exact statement in Genesis, "And God said, let there be Light." Also take note of the following. The word "form" and the word "create" are used interchangeably in the Bible. An example of this is found in Genesis 1:27 which reads "So God created man in His own image..." When we go to Genesis 2:7, it is stated in the following way: "And the LORD God formed man of the dust of the ground,..." Therefore, God spoke light into existence. Along with this, it is reasonable to conclude (as stated in Hebrews 11:3) that all the worlds were "framed" by the spoken word of the Lord. In light of this, we can use the same phrase that is stated at the beginning of Hebrews 11:3, "Through faith, we understand..." that God spoke all things into existence and to take comfort, with confidence, to express it in this manner.

There are some, who have concluded, that because there was no sun for the first three days, therefore this provides support to their "day/age" hypothesis. Indeed, the sun was not the source of the light for the first three days. Yet God provided a temporary light source from which God stated as His conclusion, (with this light source that) the evening and the morning was the 1st day (the 2nd

day & the 3rd day). In other words, night-time and day-time established what God called the 1st day, 2nd day & 3rd day. An additional explanation about the temporary source of "Light" for the first three days is documented in 2nd Cor. 4:6, "For God, who commanded the light to shine out of darkness…" He commanded "let there be light," and light came forth out of darkness. The sun was not that light source which God commanded to shine out of darkness. This light source was created for the purpose of establishing night and day which would be for establishing the passage of time. On day-1, darkness was created before light and at a point later (12 hours later) light was created. This is, no doubt, why God said, "And the evening and the morning was the 1st day," as oppose to saying, "the morning and the evening was the 1st day." Verse 16 provides the rationale for the purpose of the greater light and the lesser light, i.e. "…the greater light to rule the day and the lesser light to rule the night." The "lesser light" was used for the evening and the "greater light" was used for the morning. Let me say it in a different way, "night-time" begins in the evening and "day-time" begins in the morning. Hence darkness, which was called night, existed before light, which was called day. Darkness was created before light therefore the beginning of creation was in the evening of the first day. It seems correct to assume that approximately twelve hours after the creation of "Darkness & Waters," "Light" was created in the morning of the first day. Then, "the evening and the morning was the first day," as decreed by the Lord God. In other words, the evening (night-time) & the morning (day-time) is a 1st solar day.

GOD'S CREATION
THE 1ST DAY

QUESTIONS TO CONSIDER

1. Is Genesis one, describing the actual beginning of creation?
2. What would earth look like if it had a form?
3. What would earth look like if it was formless or without form?
4. What was the reason, given by God, for the creation of darkness?

> **Genesis 1:2 thru 5**
> ²And the earth was without form and void, and darkness was upon the face of the deep. And the Spirit of God moved upon the face of the waters.
> ³And God said, Let there be light: and there was light.
> ⁴And God saw the light, that it was good: and God divided the light from the darkness.
> ⁵And God called the light Day, and the darkness He called Night. And the evening and the morning was the first day.

Let us assume, for a moment, that God is literally describing the very beginning of creation in Genesis chapter one. On the 1st day, God's creation consisted of literal water, literal darkness and literal light. (We will not complicate this portrait by bringing in the concepts of spiritual light, spiritual waters or spiritual darkness.) With the creation of Darkness, Waters and Light, this can be identified as the creation of "space, time, and matter (& some of the laws of physics – for the existence & maintenance of waters in a liquified state)." **When we view "darkness and waters" as components which were intentionally created for the stated purpose that God indicated; just as God was purpose specific with the creation of "light;" this will dispel the concept of chaos and judgment as the rationale for the existence of waters & darkness. This then forces us to look at the creation of darkness & light as being the components designed for that which God said they were** (i.e. "the Darkness" He called "Night," & the "Light" He called "Day")**.**

In that God called the darkness night, that would mean that it was created for that purpose. The creation of "darkness & light" provides the "contributing components" for establishing time, and the creation of the "waters" establishes it as the first form of matter. I will attempt to define "space, time and matter," in a manner that I consider to be very simplistic. Although time may be the most difficult, of the three, to define.

A New Creation Model

Concerning space, it is reasonable to conclude that initially God created a limited amount of space (on the 1st day) with an intent to occupy it with the waters, and the waters would be the first form of matter. Darkness was used to establish the beginning of time. With the staggered creation of light, both darkness and light provide the contributing components for establishing time. Time can also be defined as a nonspatial continuum that is measured in terms of events that succeed one another. Time can also be explained as an irreversible succession from the past, thru the present and into the future. I am sure that there are more technical or scientific terms in which to define time, but this basic definition will do.

I will attempt to accurately visualize that which the Scriptures are portraying, during the creation week. As I do such, my intent is to remain true to the biblical descriptions. I ask that you also picture this with me. As we examine the initial conditions of the creation week, it is important for us to understand what the conditions are today. For example, under the present conditions of outer space, the laws of physics are fully operational. The behavior of water in space with its zero-gravity environment are: water will both boil and freeze; water will form spheres; and water will not drip in space. We also understand that water requires both a certain range of pressure and a certain range of temperatures to remain in a liquid phase. Recognizing that the initial conditions at the start of the creation week did differ as the creation week progressed, therefore we can make some reasonable assumptions.

During the first day of creation, the laws of physics could not have been functioning fully. Most likely there were limited functions. Yet, I think that even on the third day, such was still partially operating because the earth was the only planet in the entire universe. Keep in mind that these laws would be established and initiated by God. On the first day, the initial condition defined by the Scripture is that all of the available space contained water. With that in mind, we find that the Scriptures describe the water as being in a liquid phase. I cannot say that I understand the physics which were specific to the waters during the first two days of creation, but my choice is to trust the narrative described in the Scriptures. I will speculate on the possible initial conditions specific to the early stages of the creation of water, darkness, light and the firmament.

Consider the following. On the evening of the first day (when God began creating), the first two items created were waters and darkness. These items occupied all of the existing space that God created for them. There was not a sun nor any astronomical objects that would function as a mechanism to generate or to transfer heat. Without such, heat gain or loss through radiation would not exist. The condition which we today refer to as the vacuum of space most likely did not exist. It was not until the 2nd day that additional space was created. The laws of physics (on the

A New Creation Model

1st & 2nd day of creation) were not operational or maybe I should say that only some of the laws were operating. Perhaps I can say, there existed only the physical laws that were necessary for water to maintain its liquid state. As a reminder, when light was created on the 1st day, it was not light from the sun. With these things in mind, the Bible referred to this substance as being (liquid) waters. The text did not say that the Spirit of God moved upon the surface of the ice or the surface of the vapors but the surface of the waters. So, all of the "space" that existed on the 1st day was occupied by "waters." I believe it is reasonable to conclude that on the first day, the initial conditions and/or temperature of the waters were uniform throughout all the available space of which waters occupied. The Spirit of God moved upon the face (or surface) of the waters, and not just on a small portion of its surface. As a reminder, every centimeter of space that existed on day 1, contained water.

Throughout this book, I have two types of illustrated models for the creation account. The two models differ in silhouette and design with an intent to portray the possible appearance of our universe, as each day progress. These provide a type of visual aid as we seek to comprehend the word image that the Scriptures describe.

GOD'S CREATION THE 1ST DAY

**Model-1 "Waters" everywhere
A view of all of creation on the 1st Day**

**Model-2 "Waters" everywhere
A view of all of creation on the 1st Day**

GOD'S CREATION THE 2ND DAY

A QUESTION TO CONSIDER:

1. Did God identify the "waters above" as liquid or as vapors?
2. Does Genesis only describe the creation of the earth or the universe also?
3. Were the sun, moon and the stars – all the celestial bodies - placed (at a later time) in the very same Firmament / Heaven that God created on the 2nd day?

> **Genesis 1:6 thru 8**
> [6]And God said, Let there be a firmament in the midst of the waters, and let it divide the waters from the waters.
> [7]And God made the firmament and divided the waters which were under the firmament from the waters which were above the firmament: and it was so.
> [8]And God called the firmament Heaven. And the evening and the morning were the second day.

It is portrayed in all of the traditional creation models that the waters of Day-1, is the earth and the firmament on Day-2 as the atmospheric section of the earth. Yet I maintain that the Scriptural model's description of Day-2, does not support that view. The "Firmament or the Expanse" was created as a huge vast empty area of space. God named this vast area of space as "Heaven." We have to determine if this firmament is the atmospheric section of the earth or if it is outer space. This can be determine based upon additional information provided in this chapter. I maintain that this "Heaven" which God created on the second day, is what we called "outer space." On the second day, that "outer space" was an empty Universe. Possessing no sun, no moon, no stars and no galaxies. It was not the atmospheric portion of the earth with clouds. For it was the same "firmament / heaven" in which God placed all of the cosmological systems, on the 4th day. In verse 20 of chapter 1, the KJV used the following wording for the flight domain of the fowl of the earth as "…the open firmament of heaven". Also, a notation in my Bible presents the actual Hebrew wording where the fowl of the air are to fly in as: "… **face of the firmament of heaven**,". This Hebraic phrase is significant; for I believe that it provides insight for us to properly understand which section God was referring to by His use of the word firmament (in Gen. 1:6). Since God referred to the "flight section for birds" as the "face of the firmament of heaven," that would mean that His use of the word "firmament" (for that which He created on day-2), **was not with an intent to describe the atmospheric**

section of earth. The **"face of it"** is descriptive of the section relative to heaven. The only reasonable conclusion would be that the reference to the "face of it" is descriptive of the atmospheric section of earth. God called the firmament "Heaven." Therefore, it seems reasonable to say, it was "outer space" that was created on day-2; and not the portion of the heaven in which the fowls were designated to fly in. For God referred to that as the **"face of the firmament of heaven."** {Rhetorically speaking: What is the common understanding of the adage which articulates "the face of a thing"? If I were to tell you that I have placed an object near the "face of the Lincoln Memorial Monument," would you look for that object at the front of it, inside of it or at the back of it? At the front of it, of course. No one under this context would consider the front (or the face of it) to be the actual monument.} Therefore day-2 was not a description of what some have called the creation of the atmospheric heaven. With that in mind, this presents additional evidence that this portion of my model is beyond question in presenting day-2 creation as the entire "universal heaven." Take note that the placement of this universal expanse was right dab in the middle of that body of waters, which could not have been the earth. Certainly, the "waters" were not the earth in a flooded state, and should we say such, we would have to say that each half of the earth is on the outer portions of the universe (because God placed Heaven in the middle of the waters). Allow me to say it this way, with a sphere of water as a model for the earth (on the 1st day), and the firmament (on day-2) being the outer space (or the heavens), that would mean that the outer space was placed in the middle of the earth, on Day-2. If the firmament is in the middle of the earth, then that would place each half of the earth on the outer edges of the universe. The Scriptures clearly describe the waters as being divided by the firmament that God called heaven into two locations (above and below the firmament). Therefore, having a model which depicts the waters as being the earth, would end up with half of the earth on one side of the Universe and the other half of the earth on the opposite side of the Universe.

Scholars differ on the appropriate representation of the Hebrew word "**Raqiya**," which is translated as "firmament." The following are some of the different theories: #1 a solid dome - that is a hard firm vault; #2 that which was pounded into a thin (metal) sheet; #3 the sky or the atmospheric section around the earth; #4 an arch - that is an expanded arch or a stretch out arch; and #5 the expanse or expansion - that is a huge open or spacious area." Consider my rationale for a few moments. Selecting the concept of an "unoccupied universe" as the model for the expanse is descriptive of the space in which the cosmological systems were placed. (This is referred to as an "unoccupied universe," because on the second day there existed no stars or planetary systems occupying the universe.) If our model of the "firmament" is to be described as that which was pounded into a thin translucent metal sheet - or a type of canopy (as posit by Dr. Carl Baugh – whom I have great respect for), such a model will conflict with Gen. 1:17. Because the same Hebrew word (Raqiya) is used in reference to the "firmament" which God placed all the stars and all planetary systems in, on the fourth day.

Nevertheless, when a consideration is made of the actual Hebrew phraseology, "the face of the firmament of heaven"; this suggests that the description of the location for the term firmament (Raqiya - expressed in verse 6) is describing what is commonly called outer space. In light of these considerations, it is reasonable to conclude that the appropriate representation of the word raqiya (in reference to the creation description) should be interpreted using the simplistic term "the universal expanse" – commonly called outer space. All of the area outside of the earth's atmosphere would perhaps be a better way to clearly define that spatial expanse. Allow me to emphasize again that additional confidence in my conclusion exists because of the distinction that is made to describe the flight zone designated for the fowls; was verbally differentiated by describing the specific location relative to that "firmament" (i.e. the **face** of the firmament of heaven).

We have a perception that the position of our planet is "somewhat" near the center of this universe. I have presented two models, with which we perhaps may be able to visualize what creation looked like on day-2. When we view **Model-1** as representing "all of creation in the evening of the second day," we will see waters above and below an empty firmament. **Model-2** presents, the same scenario, in a slightly different depiction, with waters both above and below the firmament called outer space. Model-2, just may more closely resemble our present concept of the universe, yet it is difficult to determine the position of the earth relative to its location in the universe.

Model-1
A view of all of creation on the 2nd Day
Waters above & below the firmament

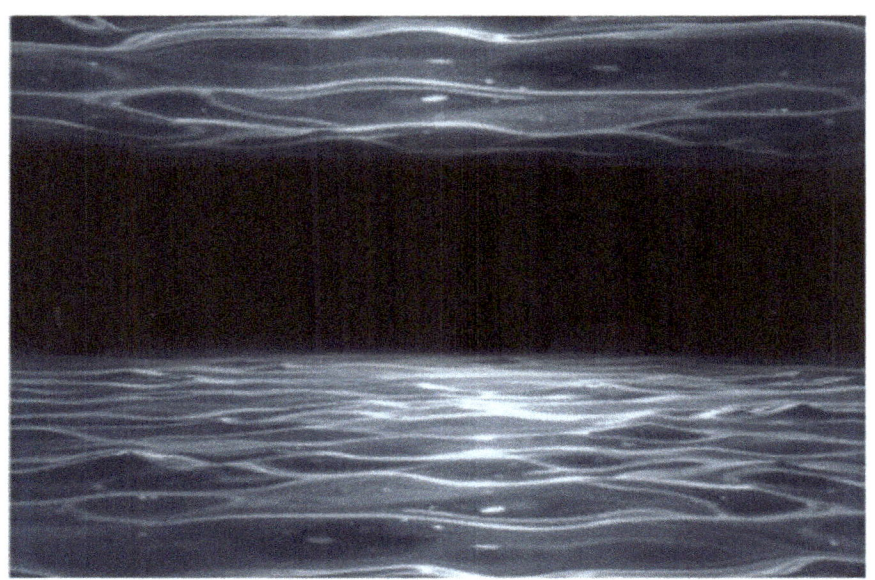

A NEW CREATION MODEL

Model-2
A view of all of creation on Day-2
Waters above & below the firmament

GOD'S CREATION THE 3RD DAY

Genesis 1:9 thru 13

⁹And God said, Let the waters under the heaven be gathered together unto one place, and let the dry *land* appear: and it was so.

¹⁰And God called the dry *land* Earth; and the gathering together of the waters called he Seas: and God saw that *it was* good.

¹¹And God said, let the earth bring forth grass, the herb yielding seed, *and* the fruit tree yielding fruit after his kind, whose seed *is* in itself, upon the earth: and it was so.

¹²And the earth brought forth grass, and herb yielding seed after his kind, and the tree yielding fruit, whose seed *was* in itself, after his kind: and God saw that *it was* good.

¹³And the evening and the morning were the third day.

As I consider my previous assertions, it seems reasonable to say that the creation of the earth took place

A New Creation Model

on the 3rd day (Genesis 1:9). God created the earth on the third day along with some living systems – that is to say, the plants, grass and herbs. The formation of the earth began, when the Lord said to the waters under the heaven, "let the waters come together into one place." {In the next paragraph, I will express a few things that I think are noteworthy about the "waters under the heaven".} Then God separated the waters, and commanded the dry land to appear. After this God said "Let the earth bring forth" grass, herb & fruit tree. The details documented in Genesis 1:9 thru 13, were created beginning at the start of night-time and concluding at the end of the day-time which God identified as the third day. As a reminder, earth was the first planet created in God's universe.

For those who enjoy their use of the NIV translation, it is worthwhile to know that the NIV translated "sky" for the Hebrew word "shamayim" throughout all of chapter one, except for the first verse. In the first verse "shamayim" is translated "heavens." My thoughts are that the word "heavens" is the better translation because it represents more accurately the description expressed in the Scriptures. Justification for my rationale was presented in the chapter titled "God's Creation The 2nd Day," with my exposition on the creation of the firmament. In the KJV & the NKJV, the Hebrew word "raqiya" is translated as "firmament" and is also translated as "expanse" in the NIV. Both are good renderings for the word "raqiya" however in Genesis 1:8, God called the firmament / expanse shamayim, which is translated 'heaven' in the KJV & 'sky' in the NIV." Typically, in the minds of most Americans, the word sky is considered the atmospheric section of the earth. The heavens are thought of as the section which we typically refer to as "outer space" or the rest of the universe. In Genesis 1:14, God said (when creating the sun, moon & stars), "Let there be lights in the expanse of the sky," according to the NIV. The reading is as follows in the KJV, "Let there be lights in the firmament of heaven". As we continue to verse 17, the Scripture states that God set the lights in the firmament of heaven (KJV) or in the expanse of the sky (NIV). It is a reasonable conclusion to say that the sun, moon and stars are not in the atmospheric section of the earth. All creation models that I have seen in my lifetime have portrayed the expanse of day-2 as being the limited atmospheric section of the earth; and have identified the "waters above the expanse" as cloud vapors or evaporation of waters. For what it is worth to you, these are my reasons for stating that the word heaven appears to be a more suitable rendering. The firmament was & is what we call the outer space. On day-3 this huge firmament was completely empty. As my model indicates, on the outer edge of this universe or on the outer edge of our firmament exists the "waters above the firmament." I believe that Psalms 148:4 testifies to this reality. "Praise him, ye heavens of heavens, and ye waters that be above the heavens." I think that model-2 provides perhaps the best illustration which is consistent with Genesis chapter one and with Psalms 148:4.

Here is something to give thought to. For some things, there is more than one way to express the same action or the same end result. For example, God said, "Let the earth bring forth grass ... *and* the fruit tree...," and there was grass & fruit tree. If I were to restate what just took place, I would not be incorrect to express it in the following manner. On the third day, God created (or spoke into existence) grass and the fruit trees. As we consider verse 20 which used the exact same wording by stating "Let the waters bring forth abundantly the moving creature that hath life...". Then verse 21 express what took place in verse 20 by stating, "And God <u>created</u> great whales and every living creature that moveth,... and every winged fowl..." this statement defines what took place in verse 20. From which we can conclude that the mere act of God saying, "Let it bring forth" is indeed the act of creating. Hence this clearly grants that God's proclamation, in effect, creates. When God said, "let the dry *land* appear and let the earth bring forth grass & fruit tree," ...the land, the grass and the fruit tree had not been there previously. Another point to make is to say, we should not forget the context of Genesis one. It is (contextually) the account of the beginning; the account of "Who did what & when." All things were created by God's proclamations. As affirmed in Psalms 33:6 & 9 "By the word of the Lord were the heavens made; and all the host of them by the breath of His mouth. For He spake, and it was done; He commanded, and it stood fast." This is God's method of creating.

With these things in mind, I will present the additional details which Genesis chapter 2 verses 4 thru 9 provides for us concerning the 3rd & 6th day of creation. Verse 4 uses language to remind of us of the creation week; verses 5 thru 9 directs us to the 3rd and the 6th day of creation thru reminding us what was created on these two days. By providing us with an account of the conditions before the plants & herbs grew or came forth and before God created a man to till the ground. God watered "the face of the whole ground" with a mist. "And out of the ground made the Lord God to grow every tree that is pleasant to the sight, and good for food…" This growth was rapid growth, I do believe. And we know that on the 6th day, God created man both male & female.

A New Creation Model

Model-2: With Day-3, Model-1 ceases to be a good depiction of the creation model. I am using the next two diagrams as a visual aid & have identified both as Model-2.

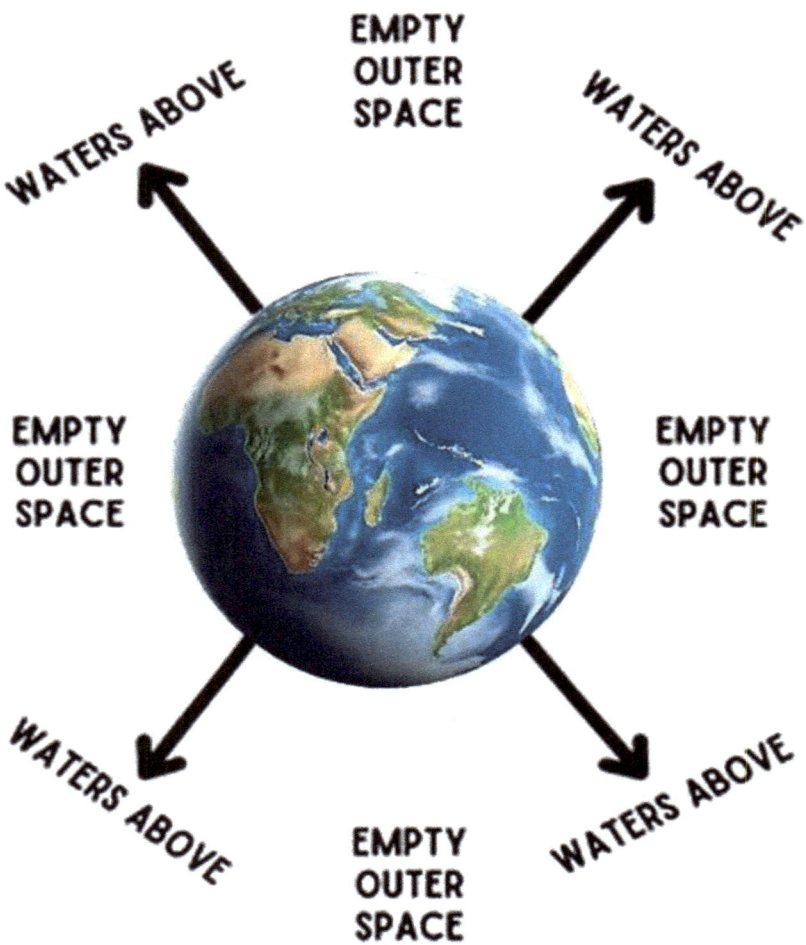

Model-2: The earth is enlarged relative to the universe, to display the previous Day-3 model. This model displays a visual illustration of waters above in all directions.

GOD'S CREATION
THE 4TH DAY

Genesis 1:14 thru 19

¹⁴And God said, Let there be lights in the firmament of the heaven to divide the day from the night; and let them be for signs, and for seasons, and for days, and for years:

¹⁵And let them be for lights in the firmament of the heaven to give light upon the earth: and it was so.

¹⁶And God made two great lights; the greater light to rule the day, and the lesser light to rule the night: *he made* the stars also.

¹⁷And God set them in the firmament of heaven to give light upon the earth.

¹⁸And to rule over the day and over the night, and to divide the light from the darkness and God saw that *it was* good.

¹⁹And the evening and the morning were the fourth day.

This is the day that God created all of the cosmological systems. {Allow me to present a speculative opinion – This fourth day is also the day when the remaining laws of physics became fully operational (that which is referred to as Classical Mechanics) – with exclusion of the "2nd Law of Thermodynamics", which is "Entropy = the gradual decline into disorder or deterioration – everything in the universe eventually moves from order to disorder". Creation became subjected to entropy (the introduction of the 2nd Law of Thermodynamics), at the fall of man. Entropy is expressed in Romans 8:20 & 21 in the form of the "bondage of corruption".} To be consistent with Scripture, "Entropy" could only have come into effect after the fall of man. Before the fourth day, there was not a sun nor planetary systems revolving around a sun – and there were no galactic systems anywhere in the universe. With the creation of each celestial and terrestrial bodies (as well as with the creation of all living systems), it seems reasonable to conclude that the operational principles and laws governing their boundaries and purpose were established on the day that each were created. On the fourth day these stellar systems begin to be for "signs, and for seasons, and for days and years and to give light upon the earth." Take note that the text stated to give light upon the earth and not just to be lights in the heavens. All of the star systems and the galaxies in the entire known and unknown universe were created with earth as its focus. This is just one among the many Scriptural indicators, which suggest that God's focus was on the earth. The earth was central to God's creation plan. As with the other days, this day began in the night-time and was complete at the end of the day-time and God identified this as the fourth day. Expressing the days in terms such as night-time and day-time helps to clarify evening and morning as being a solar day.

Model-1 the 4th day of creation of God's creation
God created the Sun, Moon, Stars, Galaxies, placed them in the firmament. Again model-1 does not allow waters above, in all directions.

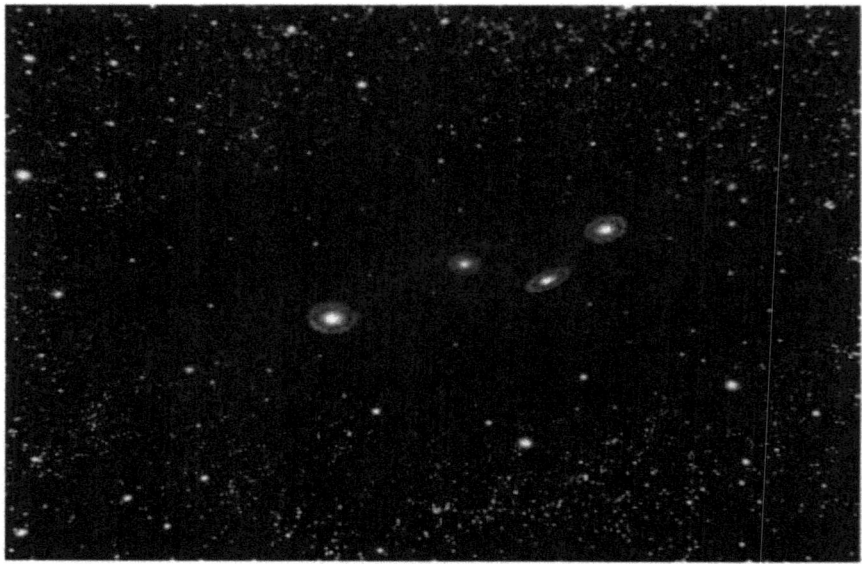

Model-2 the 4th day of creation

This model represents the entire universe with waters above the heavens as specified in Psalms 148:4

This model represents the entire universe with waters above the heavens as specified in Psalms 148:4

TRANSLATION EXPLANATION

The following example (in a simplistic way) displays how the selection of a definition for the translation of a word is made. A definition that will render a meaning that is contextually fitting, in order to convey the intended thought, when assigning denotation or connotation in the translation of a language. As an example, I will use the Hebrew word "shamayim (pronounced – sha-mah-yim)," which is translated "heaven." Throughout the Scriptures, the word heaven has the following meanings: 1) The abode of the stars; 2) The visible universe; 3) The sky; 4) The atmosphere; *and* 5) The abode of God. I will use (as an example) a text in Genesis 7:23 of which God speaks of the destruction of the "fowl of the heaven" during the flood of Noah. I will ask you, which meaning of the word heaven applies to this text? We know that the fowl do not fly in the "abode of the stars" or in "the visible universe" nor in "the abode of God." The meaning that should be assigned is the sky or the atmospheric heaven. That decision was made based upon the text indicating certain earthly creatures whose flight domain is in heaven (the area of heaven with oxygen in the atmosphere – a part of earth); such deductive reasoning is dependent upon the context for a correct denotation. By this type of deduction, we can select the applicable meaning. In some cases, clarification for the contextual interpretation of a word is not fully established until several verses beyond the place where the word initially appeared. For example, the word "firmament," which God renamed "heaven." This word first appeared in chapter 1, verse 6, and one could conclude that verse 6 is to be interpreted as the atmospheric section of earth which we typically call the sky. Yet, a more suitable meaning was established from additional context usage which was found when reading verses 6 thru 20. The latter verse described a more specific section of the firmament with its use of a phrase which identified a distinction between earth's atmosphere and heaven, by using the term "the face of the firmament of heaven." This phrase identified earth's sky as oppose to the section beyond, which we normally refer to as heaven or outer space.

If at this point you have been persuaded by this new creation model, you do not have to read further. However, in the event that what has been presented has not been with enough clarity, simplicity or textual persuasiveness to establish the validity of this model; consider the last chapter titled "**A Verbal Sketch**." {In the event you are not born again, this "Salvation Message" is written for you. Please read and consider accepting Jesus.} The purpose of "A Verbal Sketch" is to explain this model using a simplistic "word-picture" (to paint with words). When a concept is presented with less details and in a less complex manner, it is a better approach for some people.

SALVATION MESSAGE

"Repent and believe the Gospel." God is offering you a chance to start over, a chance to change your life and your lifestyle. This opportunity for change has been provided to us through the life, death and resurrection of Jesus Christ. Our problem is not a lack of goodness or good deeds. We have a problem with consistency. We are not consistently good. Sometimes we can be the sweetest person there is. At times you can be the sweetest person there is. You can at times, impress others with your niceness and your thoughtfulness. Is that not true? So much so that a compliment is made about you in the words of, "I wish everyone were as nice as you." Yet the reality is, you are not nice like that all the time. For this reason, we are sinners, you are a sinner and do fall short of pleasing God by your works/deeds. For this reason, you cannot identify yourself as being good consistently. We would not feel as bad if our failures only occur once in our lifetime, but such happens many times. For most of us, it is a daily occurrence, day after day, week after week, month after month and year after year. You will, at some point, realize that you are a "wretched man," as stated in Romans 7:24. You will ask, "Who shall deliver me from this body of death?" Who will deliver me from this sinful body? In other words, who will help me to get out of this cycle of sin, this cycle of doing wrong? Deliverance is obtained through Jesus Christ. If you are exhausted from your cycle of sin and desire to have a good conscience towards God. If you want your conscience to be "void of offense towards God and towards men." This can be obtained, today – right now – by repenting and giving your life to God, through Jesus Christ. This can happen with words as simple as saying "God forgive me of my sins and come into my life and save me." By turning to God in this manner, God will both forgive you and change you and provide you with a "start over." Through which you will also obtain eternal life. If you want this change in your life, just repent now as I pray with you. (This is my prayer for you.) Lord, for those who have prayed this prayer, forgive them and cleanse them of their unrighteousness, and allow a new start in their lives. Lift the weight of sin from their conscience, in Jesus' name. Amen. With this, you are saved.

"WHY CALL ME GOOD," SAID JESUS

There is a certain event recorded in the Scriptures (Matt. 19:16 & 17) in which a young man came to Jesus, addressing Jesus by saying, "Good Master, what good thing shall I do, that I may have eternal life?" Jesus' immediate response was, "Why callest thou me good? there is none good but one, that is, God."

I had often wondered, why Jesus excluded himself when He stated that there was none good but God. At that time in my mind, if anyone should be labeled as good,

Jesus would be at the top of the list. It was not until years later that I came to understand the reason why Jesus did not include Himself. The answer is found in the Apostle Paul's teaching on obtaining righteousness by the Law. In that, he taught that if a man keeps the Law but offends it at one point, he would still be guilty of breaking the entire Law. The point of it is, if a person was to be righteous based upon the Law, that person could only obtain righteousness by keeping the Law flawlessly consistent. I would be able to keep the Law for a short period of time but not for a "lifetime." In order for me to obtain righteousness in the sight of God by the Law, I would have to keep the Law from birth till death without breaking it. The Scripture written in Hebrews 5:15 states that Jesus, "… was in all points tempted like as we are, yet without sin." This statement was not written and could not have been written until after Jesus' death. The Scripture declared Jesus as being without sin, after He had lived without sin from birth to death. Therefore, Jesus rightly stated, at that time in His life, "there is none good but one (God)."

A VERBAL SKETCH

MODEL OUTLINE:
EACH DAY REGARDED AS A 24-HOUR PERIOD

Day-1: Creation of Time – (the beginning) waters, darkness and light

Day-2: Creation of Heaven – an empty universe without celestial bodies

Day-3: Creation of Earth – (1st planet) Land, seas & botanical living systems

Day-4: Cosmic creation – Sun, planets, stars & Laws of Physics completed

"'In the beginning God created…' is a phrase to specify that God had created nothing previously (St Augustine)." Therefore, before God created anything, there was "nothing," absolutely nothing with the exclusion of the **LORD GOD HIMSELF** – that is to say, the Godhead. Perhaps, a good question to ask at this point is: What does "nothing" look like? Nothing can be very difficult to describe. One way that I can describe nothing is to say that "nothing is no-thing." Nothing is the nonexistence of everything that I can and cannot both mentally and visually comprehend. "Nothing" would be the nonexistence of all things. Colossians 1:16 is a presentation of the opposite of nothing. "For by Him were all things created, that are in heaven, and that are in earth, visible and invisible, whether

A New Creation Model

they be thrones, or dominions, or principalities, or powers: all things were created by Him..." Therefore, nothing would be the absence of these things. I stated all of that to establish the reasonableness of my next statement. The initial starting point of a creation model should begin with "nothing," that is to say, that which existed before God begin creating anything. When there was no space, no time, no water, no darkness and no physical light. A model with a starting point of "nothing" will help to develop a more visually accurate portrait and a better appreciation for the details of every individual component created on each day of the creation week.

Day-1

On the first day, most creation models present the earth as a suspended sphere of water (in a system-less firmament), but be aware that the text states the firmament did not exist on the first day. The "firmament" was not created until day-2. This indicates that most models do not depict creation, as close as possible to the model represented in Genesis 1 on day 1. Consider the following statement. The amount of space or area that the "waters" occupied on day-1 was certainly not the spacious firmament that God named heaven. Picture (if you will) "waters & darkness" as the only two substances that can be seen in any direction that you would look, on the first day before the creation of light. This is assuming that you could see in the dark. Better still, after the creation of light, if you were to look in every direction - on day 1, there would have been "waters" in every square inch of existing space. Is that not true? {Take note that there was no physical space unoccupied by "waters," on day-1. It may be very difficult to visualize a time when that which we call outer space did not exist, but there was a point before creation at which "time and space" did not exist. **Keep in mind that God did not and does not need space to exist in**. God is non-spatial – God exists outside of what we understand as space.} Draw an illustrated picture of all of creation being filled with just water (on day-1). Take a sheet of paper and picture that this sheet represents everything that was created on day one. The whole sheet would be covered with just "waters." We cannot say, with any certainty, that the "waters" possessed a spherical shape at that point. The "expanse," that is commonly called outer space, had not been created on Day-1. Therefore, the effect of the physical properties of "space" on waters is not relevant. To be more specific, the "surface tension effects," that the vacuum of space has on waters, most likely did not exist on the first day. Also remember this fact; waters alone filled every iota of existing space on Day-1. There was no additional space until God created "additional space" on the 2nd day, which He called the firmament. (We cannot be sure that there was a vacuum environment – on the (first) day when God created the waters. A first day that is void of any stellar or planetary systems may be difficult for us to envision. Yet the narrative given by the Bible presents such a portrait. Also, on day-1 that which we call gravity most likely did not exist.) Consider the possibility that the text of verse 2, **is not** referring to "the waters" as being the earth. In verse two, the first phrase may possibly be with the intent to only describe what was not there. Allow me to ask you this: If you were to describe a pre-earth condition on the first day, how would you do it, if you wanted to convey that your ultimate focus is the earth? How would you express such using a short description? Well, I think that God did an excellent job. In that God said "… the earth was without form and void..:" The descriptive definition of these two words (without form and void), may also infer that there was nothing there. At that point, the earth had not been formed – the earth had not been created. In the electronic version of the Strong's Concordance, you will find 14 English translations of the Bible, under the "Bible" tab., when referencing the Hebrew word "tohuw:" 5 versions used the word **formless**; 5 used the word **without form**; 3 used the word **waste** and 1 used the word **without shape**. In light of the fact that this is the account of the "beginning of creation," this establishes the context as a creation narrative. It would follow that the proper rendering of the thought that is being expressed would be a depiction with the intent to convey a visual portrait of the beginning. Therefore, a suitable meaning that depicts the earth as being "without form" or formless, is to say that the earth possessed no visible shape, no pattern and no structure on the first day. Take note of Jesus' reference to the beginning (of creation), His implication was that the beginning covered a period of six days (Mark 10:6).

Day-2

Now on your next picture, (for day-2) draw waters & a huge empty universe. In other words, draw the firmament in the midst of the waters. Again, if we posit that the waters (expressed in verse 2) as being the earth flooded with water; or that this was the initial formation of the earth during the first day, then this huge expanse which was placed in the midst (middle) of the waters will push each half of the earth on opposite sides of the universe. Yet some have tried to interpret verses 6, 7 & 8 as the creation of earth's atmospheric section called the sky. If this is our portrait of earth, we will also have difficulty with verse 17, which states that the cosmic systems are placed into earth's small "atmospheric section," on the fourth day. Nonetheless, (again) we must not forget that the Hebrew phraseology of, "the face of the firmament of heaven," as presented in verse twenty, which is describing the atmospheric portion of earth, that which we call the sky. However, if we have a portrait displaying the second day as God creating the vast (vacant) heaven that we called the universe. This provides a realistic model which allows for an unswerving flow of interpretive thought that is consistent with the flow of the subsequent texts. We will have no missing or conflicting information when we picture verse 6 as being the huge outer space, in which all of the cosmological systems are to be placed in on the fourth day. Interpreting verse 6 as a portrait of the universal expansion also reinforces the premise that the earth had not been created. Of course, we will have to address the fact that the text affirms that there was & is "waters above the firmament." To this we can posit that "waters" exist on the outer realm of the heavens, even to this day. We find Scriptural support for this model in Psalm 148:4, "Praise Him, ye heavens of heavens, and ye waters that be above the heavens." Waters is stated as being above the heavens (not the singular word heaven). This should be sufficient, for those of us who embrace the literal-normal interpretation of the Scriptural text.

Day-3

With verse-9, it would follow that the gathering together of the waters (that are below the firmament) into one place could "also" be a description of the creation of our sphere-shaped earth. After which was the creation of "dry *land*." It seems reasonable to conclude that on the third day, the mechanism for earth's gravity was created. This would allow for the water, soil & botanical (plant) systems to be held in place. Again, I am saying that the earth was not created on day one but that verse-2 was only a descriptive portrait of pre-earth conditions. The Hebrew word "**tohuw**," which is translated "without form (KJV)" will leave us with the following choice of options as its intended meaning: formlessness, confusion, nothingness, wasteland, or a place of chaos and vanity. We will then have to choose a definition that is consistent with the context. If we trust God by accepting that He was describing the beginning of creation, that would mean that the term "in the beginning" was the intended context and represents the collective descriptions expressed in chapter one. It would therefore stand to reason that "chaos, vanity, confusion and wasteland" is not the portrait that He was painting. {We should always keep in mind the following statement as our unrelenting reflective perspective. **Throughout all the Scripture, the phrases "in the beginning, at the beginning & from the beginning" is always the terminology used as a direct reference to the six days of creation.**} In light of that, it would be unreasonable to hold to a view that there was a beginning before the beginning. Let us also consider Hebrews 11:3, "…the worlds were framed by the word of God, so that things which are seen were not made of things which do appear." Consequently, the concept of "wasteland, confusion or chaos" existing before the six days of creation is not consistent with the Genesis' narrative. Which some use to justify a Pre-Adam Creation or some refer to such as a Pre-Adam Renovation. Also, some will use it in an attempt to make the biblical time line agree with the secular world view, pertaining to the age of the earth and the universe. However, my position is that when science is unbiasedly assessed, it will not be in conflict with nor contradict the Biblical world view.

In Genesis one, God provides us with His eyewitness account of creation (it is a portrait of creation). Therefore, on day-1 the earth possessed no shape, pattern or structure, and to say that the earth was "without form," would be descriptive of God's goal to create the earth. (Again) It follows that the first portion of verse-2 is presenting, a pre-earth framework. The definition applied to that which has a **form** is to possess a shape, a pattern, a physical appearance and/or a structure; and to be without a shape, pattern, physical appearance or structure is to be "without form." We can consider such to be "formless". The word "void," by definition, means "to contain no matter; no material substance, and/or is not there." There is no indication in the translation of this text that "formless and void with waters and darkness" is indicative of chaos or judgment. Therefore, on the third day, God gathered together into one place the waters (which were below), and created dry land, plants, weeds and trees. Therefore, God commanded the waters (below) to be gathered together into one place and He commanded dry land to come into being, and created plants, weeds & trees on the third day.

Day-4

On day 4, verses 14 thru 19 present God's account of creating and populating the entire cosmological systems and setting them in motion. <u>**As it pertains to the celestial systems, it could be said, that the "Newtonian laws" became fully operational on the fourth day. If true, the fourth day would be the first day of independent systems operation for all stellar & non-stellar systems.**</u> I think that it is reasonable to deduce that Classical Mechanics was not fully implemented until the fourth day when heaven became fully populated. I also believe that

God created every cosmological system throughout the universe, to have some measure of influence on planet earth and that earth has some measure of influence on all the other celestial systems. One of the contributing factors of the Biblical account is that creation became subjected to "the bondage of corruption" at the fall of man. I believe it is correct to say that before the fall of man, there were no system collisions with asteroids, planets or stars throughout God's entire universe. All systems functioned flawlessly throughout all of creation. After the fall of man, creation became subjected to "entropy." All aspects of this theory maybe difficult to explain, yet my assumption is that God built perfection in the original design. God's perfection would mean the absence of entropy. Therefore, all imperfections that presently exists came by reason of "the fall," man's sin.

PROBLEMS WITH THIS MODEL

Without a spherical shaped model for "waters" during the first two days, the traditional concept of night & day being expressed through a type of planetary rotation; would make my model a bit more difficult for some to visualize. Not only so, but not having an earth during the first two days, may cause some to immediately reject this model in spite of the fact that my model more accurately matched the textual description. Yet, independent of the physical shape of the waters, God had created darkness and a temporary light source to establish the night and day cycle. In that the Scriptures stated that God said, the evening and the morning was the first day & etc... I therefore readily agreed with the Lord. On the 4th day God created the permanent mechanisms for nights, days, signs, seasons and years and these began operating on a systematic schedule. Therefore, with the special light source created to perform the mechanized function of night and day for the first three days of creation, it is possible that the cycle of night and day (especially during the first two days) were not dependent on a spherical shape for its end result. "Waters" was the only material substance which existed throughout all of creation on day-1 and that would mean that the water occupied every millimeter of space which existed (on the first day), despite the initial shape of the model.

This concludes my arguments.

OTHER BOOKS BY QUENCY GARDNER

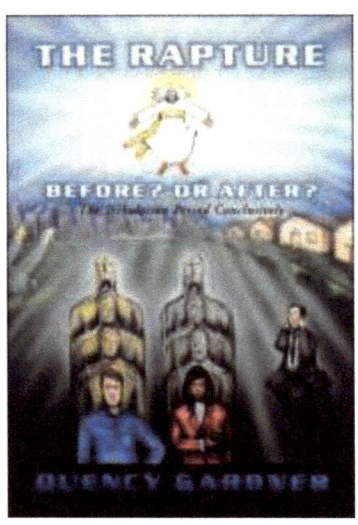
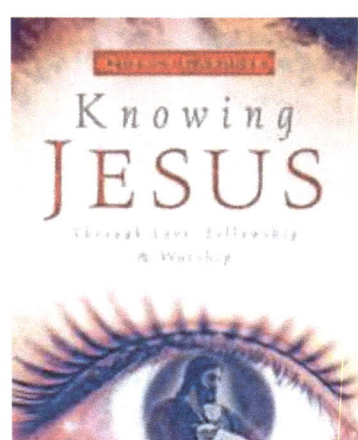

www.ingramcontent.com/pod-product-compliance
Lightning Source LLC
LaVergne TN
LVHW050137080526
838202LV00061B/6510